Canaries

and cage-birds
Illustrations

ISBN-13: 978-1495323195
ISBN-10: 1495323196

Dtp and graphic design
Iacob Adrian

This documentary book use, combined in various proportions, elements from the following categories, forms and subsets :

- documentary

- documentary photography

- feature

- journalism

- arts journalism

- visual journalism

- photojournalism

- celebrity photography

in order to :

- employ material as the object of cultural critique ,

- quote to illustrate an argument or point ,

- use material in historical sequence,

providing independent opinion,

using photos, press articles, advertisements, opinions of fans etc. ...

European
Goldfinch.

Norwich Canary,
(clear yellow,)
Natural Color.

European
Bullfinch.

Golden Spangled
Lizard Canary.

Norwich Canary.
Evenly Marked, Crested Yellow.

Nonpareil.   *Indigo Bird.*

Red Cardinal,
or Virginia Nightingale

Brazilian,
or Gray, Cardinal.

Blackcap.

European Nightingale.

Pekin Nightingale.

Red and Blue Macaw.

Red Headed Love Bird   Australian, or Shell, Paroquet.

South American Troopial.

Norwich Canary,
· *(clear yellow,)*
Natural Color.

European
Goldfinch.

European
Bullfinch

.Golden Spangled
Lizard Canary.

Norwich Canary.
Evenly Marked, Crested Yellow.

Nonpareil.　　　　　　　　　　　　　　*Indigo Bird.*

Red Cardinal,
or Virginia Nightingale

Brazilian,
or Gray, Cardinal.

European Thrush.   European Blackbird.

Blackcap.

Pekin Nightingale.

European Nightingale.

South American Troopiai.

Red and Blue Macaw.

African Gray Parrot.

Cuban Parrot.

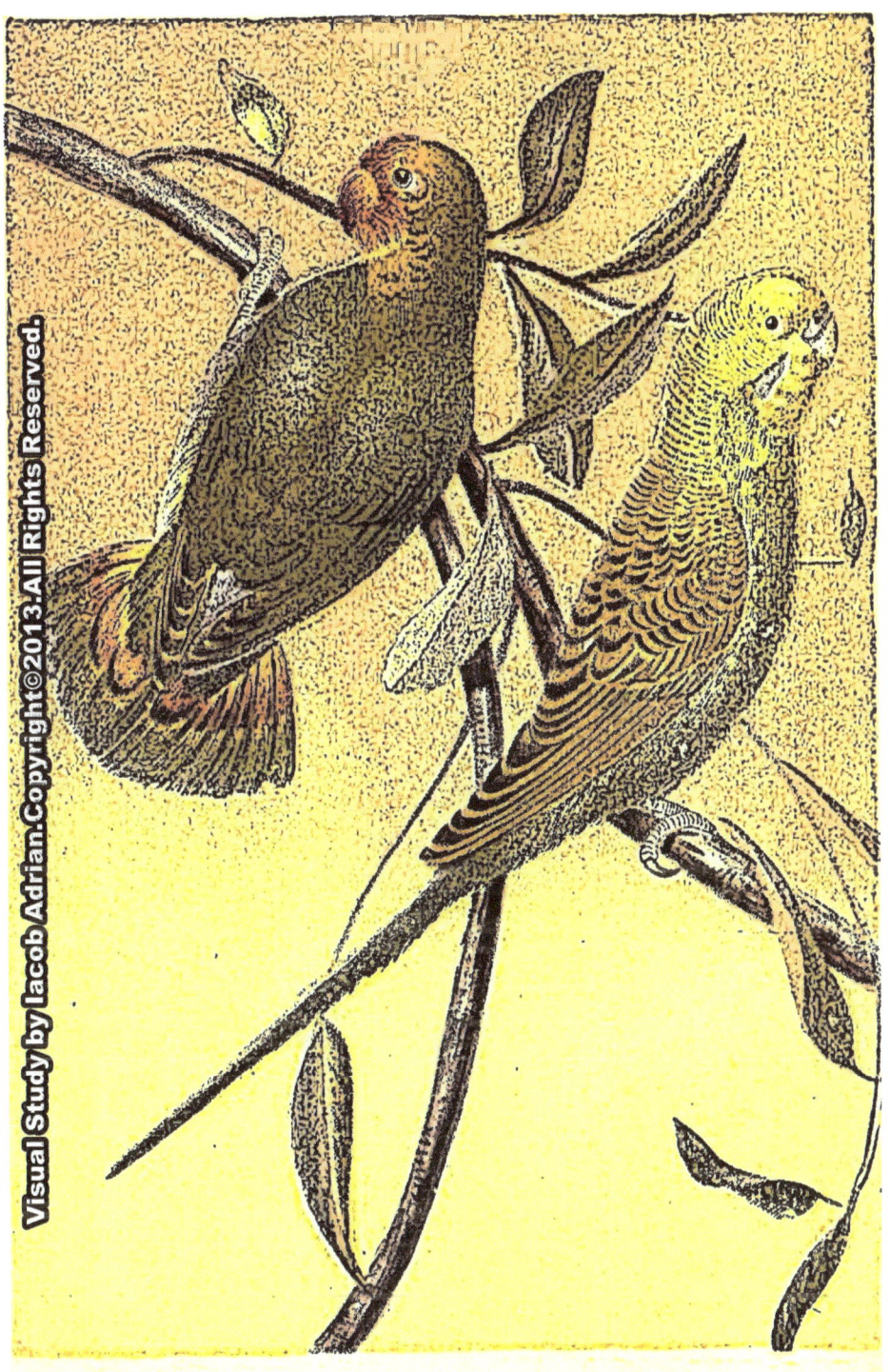

Red Headed Love Bird.   Australian, or Shell, Paroquet.

Bibliographic sources :

Canaries and cage-birds ([c1883])

Author: Holden, George Henry, 1848-1914
Publisher: New York, Boston, Mass. : G.H. Holden

Canaries and cage-birds : the food, care, breeding, diseases
and treatment of all house birds ... (c1888)

Author: Holden, George Henry, 1848-1914
Publisher: New York, Boston, Providence : G. H. Holden

www.ingramcontent.com/pod-product-compliance
Lightning Source LLC
Chambersburg PA
CBHW050930290526
45792CB00002B/963